Rob Thorpe

NEXT STEPS

Starting Your New Life in Christ

FORWARD by Bill Elliff,
Founding Pastor of the Summit Family of Churches

© All In Ministries, Inc
Little Rock, AR 72223
marriagesthatmatter@gmail.com

NEXT STEPS:
Starting Your New Life in Christ
Authored by Rob Thorpe
Forward by Bill Elliff

Copyright @ 2025 by All In Ministries, Inc.
All rights reserved.

Published by All In Ministries, Inc.
1 Piedmont Lane
Little Rock, AR 72223

All rights reserved. No part of this book may be reproduced or transmitted in any form or by any means, electronic or mechanical, including photocopying and recording, or by any information storage and retrieval system without permission in writing from the publisher.

Cover design by Chris Paxton

ISBN: 978-1-7359604-6-3

Printed in the United States of America

Most Scripture taken from the New American Standard Bible

FORWARD

There is only one thing more wonderful than coming to know Christ as your personal Savior ... coming to know Him MORE and MORE for the rest of your life and throughout eternity! In fact, the Apostle Paul said that his greatest desire was to "know Him and the power of His resurrection."

When you become a true follower of Christ and are born again, you are not merely making some changes in your life and schedule. You have a new Life inside of you—the life of Christ. Learning how to walk with Him and let Him lead every day is vital. And, you'll be growing in that understanding for the rest of your life.

The following pages will be a tremendous help to you. Rob Thorpe has discipled many people and knows how this works. He has very carefully, but very simply, given you a guide to know the foundational truths that will help you get off to a good start. Whether you are a brand-new believer or you've known Him for a good while and just need some fresh tools to know how to walk with Him, this book is for you.

I was once discipling a man who had never learned the fundamentals of the faith. He told me after a few months, "Bill, I feel like I received an amazing gift years ago, but I'm just now really opening the package and finding out what I have now that I have Christ! And it's changing my life!"

I pray that will be your testimony as well. And you couldn't have a better guide.

By God's grace,

Bill Elliff
Founding Pastor of the Summit Family of Churches
Pastor and Church Director for OneCry! A Nationwide Call for Spiritual Awakening.

TABLE *of* CONTENTS

It's Cold in Here! 7

Chapter 1 - What Just Happened? 11

Chapter 2 - Spices and Grave Clothes 17

Chapter 3 - You Are a New Creation 21

Chapter 4 - The New You 25

Chapter 5 - The New Responsibility 31

Chapter 6 - Shedding the Old Clothes 35

Chapter 7 - Teach Us to Pray 41

Chapter 8 - Tell Me About Baptism 49

Chapter 9 - Everybody Needs a Body 53

Chapter 10 - What Could Go Wrong? 57

Chapter 11 - Shots Fired! 61

Chapter 12 - The Real You 67

Chapter 13 - Time to Change Clothes 71

Chapter 14 - Let Your Light Shine 77

Chapter 15 - Now What? 83

Appendix A 87

Some Final Thoughts 89

It's Cold in Here!

It's pitch dark in here!
I can't see my hand in front of my face.
In fact, I can't see anything!
What's this stuff over my eyes, over my face?

Wait - someone's calling my name. Am I dreaming? No - there it is again - a man's voice. He is shouting my name - "Lazarus, come out !" I recognize that voice. It's my friend, Jesus.

In the eleventh chapter of the Gospel of John, we are given a firsthand account of an amazing story and an even more amazing miracle performed by Jesus......

A man named Lazarus, a friend of Jesus, was sick. He lived in Bethany with his sisters, Mary and Martha. This is the Mary who later poured the expensive perfume on the Lord's feet and wiped them with her hair (Luke 7:38). Her brother, Lazarus, was deathly sick. So the two sisters sent a message to Jesus telling him, "Lord, your dear friend is very sick."

But when Jesus received the message, he said, "Lazarus' sickness will not end in death. No, it happened for the glory of God, so that the Son of God will receive glory from this." So, although Jesus loved Martha, Mary, and Lazarus, he stayed where he was for the next two days. Finally, he said to his disciples, "Let's go back to Judea."

But his disciples objected. "Rabbi," they said, "only a few days ago, the people in Judea were trying to stone you. You can't go back there again."

Jesus replied, "There are twelve hours of daylight every day. During the day, people can walk safely. They can see because they have the light of this world. But at night, there is danger of stumbling because they have no light." Then he said, "Our friend Lazarus has fallen asleep, but now I will go and wake him up."

The disciples said, "Lord, if he is sleeping, he will soon get better!" They thought Jesus meant Lazarus was literally sleeping, but Jesus meant Lazarus had died.

So he told them plainly, "Lazarus is dead. And for your sake, I'm glad I wasn't there, for now, you will really believe. Come, let's go see him."

When Jesus arrived at Bethany, he was told that Lazarus had already been laid in his tomb for four days. Bethany was only a few miles down the road from Jerusalem, and many people had come to console Martha and Mary in their loss. When Martha got word that Jesus was coming, she went to meet him. But Mary stayed in the house. Martha said to Jesus, "Lord, if only you had been here, my brother would not have died. But even now I know that God will give you whatever you ask." Jesus told her, "Your brother will rise again." "Yes," Martha said, "he will rise when everyone else rises, on the last day."

Jesus responded, "I am the resurrection and the life. Anyone who believes in me will live, even after dying. Everyone who lives in me and believes in me will never die. Do you believe this, Martha?" "Yes, Lord," she told him. "I have always believed you are the Messiah, the Son of God, the one who has come into the world from God." Then she returned to Mary. She called Mary aside from the mourners and told her, "The Teacher is here and wants to see you." So Mary immediately went to him.

Jesus had stayed outside the village, at the place where Martha had met him. When the people who were at the house consoling Mary saw her leave so hastily, they assumed she was going to Lazarus' grave to weep. So they followed her there. When Mary arrived and saw Jesus, she fell at his feet and cried, "Lord, if only you had been here, my brother would not have died."

When Jesus saw her weeping and saw the other people wailing with her, a deep anger welled up within him (at the sorrow caused by death), and he was deeply troubled. "Where have you put him?" he asked them. They told him, "Lord, come and see." Then Jesus wept. The people who were standing nearby said, "See how much he loved him!" But some said, "This man healed a blind man. Couldn't he have kept Lazarus from dying?"

When Jesus arrived at the tomb, a cave with a heavy stone rolled across its entrance, he told the crowd, "Roll the stone aside." But Martha protested, "Lord, he has been dead for four days. The smell will be terrible."

Jesus responded, "Didn't I tell you that you would see God's glory if you believed?"

So several men rolled the stone aside. Jesus looked up to heaven and said, "Father, thank you for hearing me. You always hear me, but I said it out loud for the sake of all these people standing here so that they will believe you sent me."

Then Jesus commanded in a loud voice, "Lazarus, come out!" And his very much alive friend hobbled slowly out, his hands and feet bound in grave clothes, his face wrapped in a head cloth. (see John 11:44) Jesus told them, "Unwrap him and let him go!"

As a new believer in Christ, you too have been raised from the dead and have stepped out into a new life - a life as a Christian, a Christ-follower, a child of Almighty God. The Bible says you have been "born again", "been made alive", "passed from death to life", and called out of darkness into his marvelous light."

So now what? What do you do now that you are re-born, spiritually alive, and walking in the light of God? What are your next steps?

<u>This book is designed to help you -</u>

- better understand what has just happened to you,

- better understand what your new life as a Christian means, and

- learn how to practically begin walking with Jesus and enjoy your new life as a Christ-follower.

Welcome, dear brother or sister, to the family of God. There is much to discover, so let's get started ...

Chapter 1

WHAT JUST HAPPENED?

You may have been alone, in your room, in your car, or in your office. You may have been at church, a conference, a worship concert, or a retreat. Wherever that sacred place was, it was "your" place - it was "your" time. Your spirit said "yes" to a message about Jesus, salvation, eternal life, and, like Lazarus, you heard something. Something deep within your spirit was stirred, and you responded by asking Jesus to come into your life, to be the Lord of your life, to forgive you, to change you, save you, and make your life new. And, you know what? He did! You may have said a prayer, but your words were not as important as your heart turning to trust Him instead of yourself. From that miraculous moment, your life changed - both in the present and for all eternity.

Your First Step - Go get a Bible that you can understand - consider the English Standard Version (ESV), Christian Standard Version (CSV), or New American Standard Bible (NASB) - and let's discover what has happened and what happens next. No kidding - get a "real", paper Bible (not your phone, iPad, etc.). It is completely okay to write notes and thoughts in your Bible, and to underline or highlight verses/passages that speak deeply to you as you read. You will be glad you did in the years ahead.

Open to Ephesians, Chapter 2 in the New Testament - we will come back to this passage many times throughout the book, so more of it will make sense along the way.

And <u>you were dead</u> in your trespasses and sins, in which you used to walk when you conformed to the ways of this world and of the ruler of the power of the air, the spirit who is now at work in the sons of disobedience. All of us also lived among them at one time, fulfilling the cravings of our flesh and indulging its desires and thoughts. Like the rest, we were by nature children of wrath.

But because of His great love for us, God, who is rich in mercy, made us alive with Christ even when <u>we were dead</u> in our trespasses. It is by grace you have been saved! And God raised us up with Christ and seated us with Him in the heavenly realms in Christ Jesus, in order that in the coming ages He might display the surpassing riches of His grace, demonstrated by His kindness to us in Christ Jesus.

For it is by grace you have been saved through faith, and this not from yourselves; it is the gift of God, not by works, so that no one can boast. For we are God's workmanship, created in Christ Jesus to do good works, which God prepared in advance as our way of life. (Ephesians 2:1-10)

Like Lazarus, you and I were dead. Not physically dead, but spiritually dead. We were living our lives void of God's presence, direction, and influence. These verses remind us that we were "conformed to this world, living under the influence and control of our arch enemy (Satan), and indulging our own fleshly desires."

Dead people don't seek God or care to know Him. In fact, we were considered God's enemies -

For if, while <u>we were God's enemies</u>, we were reconciled to him through the death of his Son, how much more, having been reconciled, shall we be saved through his life! (Romans 5:10)

Even if you were a nice person and did some nice things for people in the past, the Bible tells us that, without Jesus as the Lord of our lives, all of our "good" works amount to nothing. No one deserves to go to heaven on their own merits.

There is <u>no one righteous</u>, not even one; there is n<u>o one who understands</u>; there is <u>no one who seeks God</u>. All have turned away, they have together become worthless; there is <u>no one who does good</u>, not even one. (Romans 3:10-12)

So understand this - before becoming a Christian, you were physically alive but spiritually dead, separated from the life of God. In addition, you were an enemy of God and totally incapable of seeking God or doing anything good for God or deserving of heaven.

BUT GOD.

Look back up to the passage from Ephesians, Chapter 2…

> ***But*** *because of His great love for us,* ***God****, who is rich in mercy, <u>made us alive</u> with Christ even when we were dead in our trespasses. <u>It is by grace you have been saved!</u> And God raised us up with Christ and seated us with Him in the heavenly realms in Christ Jesus, in order that in the coming ages He might display the surpassing riches of His grace, demonstrated by His kindness to us in Christ Jesus. For it is <u>by grace you have been saved through faith</u>, and this not from yourselves; it is <u>the gift of God, not by works</u>, so that no one can boast.*

You did nothing to deserve your salvation. You were dead, remember? And, by His grace and mercy, God made you alive. Like Lazarus, Jesus came to you, and He called your name. God loved you so much that He sent Jesus to pay the penalty for your sin by suffering a brutal death by crucifixion on a Roman cross. You did nothing to deserve such a sacrifice. The Bible tells us that this was God's gift to you.

Jesus came to you while you were dead. You weren't seeking Him; He was seeking you. Spiritually speaking, Jesus had the heavy stone (covering) to your grave (spiritually lifeless heart/life) rolled out of the way so light could enter your heart and you could hear His voice calling your name.

Because you were dead, you had no ability to get up and remove the huge weight of sin and guilt that affects us all, and our ability to hear God's voice. He did it all!

What do I mean by that exactly?

1. The Bible is clear that before Christ, we were "dead in our trespasses and sins."(Ephesians 2)

2. Our "dead" condition was not a result of anything we had done, or had not done, in our lives. We are all born sinners. We are all born into sin because of the sin of the first man created by God, Adam. (Romans 5:12)

3. We are also told that the "wages" (results, consequences) of our sin is eternal separation from God, or spiritual death. (Romans 6:23).

4. We are born into this world as sinners, separated from God, and are spiritually dead towards Him. Because we are dead, we have no interest in God, are not seeking God, and cannot hear God's voice or understand His Word. (Romans 8:7-8, 1 Corinthians 2:14)

5. **BUT GOD** made us alive, out of His great love and mercy. (Ephesians 2)

He has rescued us from the kingdom of darkness and transferred us into the kingdom of His dear Son, who purchased our freedom and forgave our sins. (Colossians 1:13-14)

Do you see that? It is truly by the grace of God that you are now a believer in Jesus - a Christian - a child of the King.

You didn't "find" Jesus. He found you.

So, what "did" you do?

Back to our friend, Lazarus.

Cold, dead, smelly Lazarus was lying in his tomb. All of a sudden, he was "awakened" by the voice of Jesus, and light entered his darkness.

"Lazarus, come forth!"

You and I had similar experiences, but maybe not so physically dramatic. Our cold, dead, smelly, sinful, selfish hearts were exposed to the light of the Good News, (the gospel) of Jesus. Our spirit came alive as we heard the voice of our Savior, calling our name.

But then, like Lazarus, there was a decision to be made.

Do I respond? Do I walk down the aisle of this church and speak to the pastor or church leader? Do I, in the moment, get on my knees and pray whatever comes to my mind and ask Jesus to be the Lord and Savior of my life?

However you did it, *you did it*. You responded to the voice of Jesus "by faith" and decided to walk out of the tomb of sin and death. And, according to the Bible, you now are a child of God, a believer, a joint heir with Christ, a child of God - a Christian.

Hallelujah!

But wait ... Why do you still feel bound by your old way of thinking and acting? Why is there a lingering aroma of your stinky old self clinging to you?

KEY TRUTH =

You were spiritually dead, and God made you alive. He chose you!

Chapter 2

SPICES & GRAVE CLOTHES

The Jews of Jesus' day prepared bodies for burial in a much different fashion than we do today. In the Book of John, Chapter 11 account, the word "wound" actually means "to bind, tie, or wind," and bodies were tightly rolled up in long strips of linen cloth. Because the Jews in that day did not practice embalming, they would pack various spices, aloes, and perfumes in between the layers of cloth to offset the strong smell of a decaying corpse. (See also Luke 23:56 and John 19:39).

So, Lazarus was a super fragrant mummy. Jesus made his body alive after four days of decay (and could have easily removed the associated stench as well), but what about the perfumes and spices? Those two smells could be quite overpowering.

Somehow (maybe a second miracle of loosening the grave clothes), Lazarus manages to sit upright and make his way to the entrance of the tomb, to the dismay of everyone present. John 11, verse 44, goes on to say *"the dead man came out, his hands and feet wrapped with strips of linen, and a cloth around his face."*

Standing before friends, family, and multiple skeptics was a true miracle. It was undeniable. The once-dead Lazarus was upright and obviously alive.

So is your story and mine - and everyone who hears the voice of a loving Savior and is brought to life by Jesus. We were truly, spiritually dead, but by His grace, we are now very much alive. We are walking miracles.

We can be forever thankful for a heavenly Father Who loved us enough to seek us out, call out to us, make us come alive, and encourage us to respond to that call.

But here's what you need to know next...

1. It takes time to unwrap your "grave clothes".

6. It takes time to get rid of the taint of your old self.

Several years ago, my wife and I would take our dog for walks at Two Rivers Park - a large, flatland park next to the Arkansas River, complete with trails, deer, geese, speeding bikers, and recreational walkers. In several strategic locations along the trails, there were signs posted to remind dog owners to keep their precious canines on a leash or face a possible fine.

My wife and I are pretty stereotypical "rule followers" (she would tell you I am much less so than she), and we would dutifully leash our racehorse disguised as a dog. We would, however, risk fines and imprisonment by letting him take off across the wild blue yonder on occasion. Other people did it, so surely we could too, right? What finally made us stop breaking the "law" was what happened the last time we let him loose. He took out across the fields, stopped several times to roll around, then dutifully returned to us when called.

Just before he made it to us, the stench made its arrival. At first, we thought he had rolled around in stagnant mud or something similar, but then it hit me. This was not mud, or water, or slime - it was death! He had found a dead, rotting animal carcass and, for some unexplainable reason, decided that it would be awesome to coat his entire body with the stench of death. He had taken "stink" to an entirely new level. Think of a vile word for stink - putrid, rotten, foul, offensive, gross, rancid, noxious - he was ALL of those.

And then we had to figure out how to get this decaying-animal-smelling creature into our car and back to our house, without ruining them both. Thank the Lord, we had an old blanket in the car. We rolled down our windows, held our breath for long intervals, and sped home. It took several days and several bathings, but the story ended well.

Point being?

He stunk. He stunk of death, and it was putrid. I can relate to Lazarus' family having second thoughts about Jesus asking him to come out of his grave after four hot, desert days.

Nothing is said in the story about the fact that in resurrecting Lazarus, Jesus may have also miraculously dispelled the overwhelming stench of death, and the almost equally pungent odor of pounds of spices, but his family and friends didn't hesitate to approach him and unwrap his grave clothes.

So - how long were you dead before Jesus invited you to "come forth?" I had been spiritually dead for some 17 years, and as a result, had the foul effects of years of darkness in my heart and life. Spiritually, I stunk. Some are fortunate enough to accept God's gift of salvation as a young child, but most of us have been lying in our spiritual tombs for decades and have a deep saturation of the stench of sin and death on us.

As you will see in the following Chapter, you have become a new creation in Christ. Not only has God called you out of spiritual darkness and into eternal life with Him, but you have also become a brand new person, spiritually speaking. You have been completely reborn spiritually, but physically and emotionally still shrouded in the trappings of your old life, with its habits, hangups, faults, and propensities toward sin.

Even though the Word tells us that we are "no longer slaves to sin". (Read Romans, Chapter 6, for a more in-depth explanation by the apostle Paul), and that sin is no longer our master - our old habits, attitudes, and selfish desires die hard. They want to hang around and keep us enslaved to their wishes. That is why I say, it will take time for these grave clothes to be unwrapped, and your new self to be fully revealed. (More on that just ahead also).

The Holy Spirit of God is living inside you right now. As you submit to Him and to the lordship of Jesus in your life, His Spirit will make his way throughout your entire being, spirit, soul, and body. This process (called sanctification) is

God's way of making you holy and more like Jesus. You will fall along the way. You will let God, others, and yourself down often - but thanks be to God, He is a merciful, forgiving, and patient Father Who is working daily in your life to grow you up into the likeness and character of His Son.

KEY TRUTH =

Your grave clothes are coming off, and the *smell* of sin and self is fading.
You are a work in progress. As you submit your life daily to Him,
read His Word, and pray, you will witness an amazing transformation
in the days, weeks, and months ahead.

Chapter 3

YOU ARE A NEW CREATION

Therefore, if anyone is in Christ, he is a new creature; the old things passed away; behold, new things have come. (2 Corinthians 5:17)

Something absolutely amazing has happened to you.
Something only God can do.

God sent His Spirit to take up residence in your spirit. Can we explain exactly how this works? Actually, no. But God says so in His Word, and we believe His Word.

If you love me, keep my commands. And I will ask the Father, and he will give you another advocate to help you and <u>be with you forever</u>— the Spirit of truth. The world cannot accept him, because it neither sees him nor knows him. But you know him, for he lives with you <u>and will be in you</u>. I will not leave you as orphans; I will come to you. Before long, the world will not see me anymore, but you will see me. Because I live, you also will live. On that day you will realize that I am in my Father, and you are in me, and <u>I am in you.</u> (John 14:15-20)

In this passage, Jesus tells us that, since he died and rose again, the Holy Spirit of God can now come and reside IN us, and no longer just be WITH us, like in the Old Testament. God's Spirit can reside in the spirit of every believer, and that is an unbelievable blessing from Him.

It may help to spend a minute discussing how God made us in the first place. You see, every one of us is created with a body, and also a soul (our mind, will, and emotions), and a spirit (our inner man/woman). God's Spirit comes to reside in our spirit at salvation. Before we are saved, our spirit is devoid of Him. Remember, Ephesians 2:1 says "we were dead" spiritually.

But if anyone does not have the Spirit of Christ, he does not belong to Him. (Romans 8:9b)

Actually, before you became a Christian, the Bible not only says you didn't belong to Christ, but that you lived under the power and influence of His enemy (and ours), Satan.

And you were dead in your trespasses and sins, in which you formerly walked according to the course of this world, according to the prince of the power of the air, of the spirit that is now working in the sons of disobedience. Among them we too all formerly lived in the lusts of our flesh, indulging the desires of the flesh and of the mind, and were by nature children of wrath, even as the rest. (Ephesians 2:1-3)

Without God inhabiting our spirit, you and I simply did what we pleased, what our flesh desired. We were mostly concerned about ourselves, what we wanted to do, and how others should treat us. We were totally self-focused. The Bible even says that nice people, doing nice things for others, are still separated from God and in need of a Savior. (See Isaiah 64:6, Ephesians 2:8-9, Titus 3:5)

Romans, Chapter 5, also tells us that we were - "sinners," "enemies of God," "separated from God" as well as spiritually dead. As a result, we were under God's judgment and condemnation - and that's not a good place to be.

This same passage also reassures us that even though we were all those things I just mentioned - "Christ died for us", "justified and saved us from the wrath of God", and reconciled us back to God the moment we accepted His salvation. That is wonderful news, isn't it?

So, back to how we are created…

Since God created us "in His image," and God is spirit (John 4:24), we are created as spiritual beings. Adam was brought to life by the breath of God, which is the breath of life. God "breathed" His breath, His spirit, into man, and he "became a living soul/being" (Genesis 2:7).

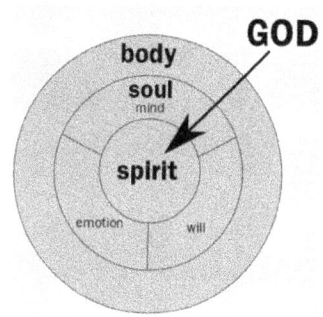

At that point, man's spirit innately had a God-consciousness that knew God's voice, fellowshipped with Him, and had a personal relationship with Him. Man's spirit was intimately connected to God.

But when man used his God-given free will to choose to disobey God, the Bible says he was "driven out of the Garden" (Genesis 3:24), and away from God's presence. In the previous chapter, God had given Adam a single restriction, a commandment not to eat of the tree of the knowledge of good and evil, "or he would surely die" (Genesis 2:17). Since Adam and Eve lived a few hundred years after eating the fruit, God was definitely not speaking of their physical death.

God was speaking of the death that would occur in Adam's spirit after disobeying Him and losing fellowship with Him. Ever since that day, mankind has been born spiritually dead, separated from God's fellowship, and deaf to His voice. That is why we are told that we are spiritually dead, slaves to sin, and enemies of God in Romans 5.

Without the Spirit of God inhabiting our spirit, we are basically spiritual zombies. We are the walking (spiritual) dead. Our bodies work, our souls are alive, but our spirits are dead, void of the presence of God we were designed to enjoy. With our spirit void of life, mankind has no other option than to be ruled by our soul - by our senses, our emotions, and our own best thoughts and ideas. I think you would agree - that hasn't turned out too well.

The amazing miracle that happens when you accept Jesus as your Savior and Lord is - you invite God's Spirit to once again take up residence in your dark, dead spirit. In an instant, your spirit becomes alive, and God's Spirit begins to change you from the very core of your being. That change begins immediately but lasts a lifetime. We will explore that much deeper in the coming chapters, but know that the Spirit that now lives in you is God Himself, and He is capable of doing amazing things in and through your life - if you allow Him and cooperate with Him.

> *For it is God Who works in you, both to will and to do of His good pleasure. (Philippians 2:13)*

KEY TRUTH =

God's Spirit now lives in you and empowers you to live a life that pleases Him and brings Him glory. We must cooperate with Him to do that.

Chapter 4

THE NEW YOU

There is an old story of an eagle egg that was accidentally knocked out of its nest during a windstorm. The neighboring poultry farmer happened upon it and placed it with the eggs of his turkeys. The young eagle, unaware of its true nature, grew up alongside the turkeys, adopting their habits and behaviors.

As he matured, the eagle began to scurry around on the ground and forage for food like the "other" turkeys, having no knowledge of his natural ability to fly. Having lost his sense of identity as an eagle, he began instead to conform to the norms of his turkey culture.

One day, the eagle heard the distant call of another eagle high in the sky, a sound he had never heard before. That call awakened something deep within the eagle, reminding him of his true nature and purpose. The eagle began to realize that he was meant for more. He felt a longing to soar through the skies, not scratch around on the ground like a turkey.

Inspired and emboldened by his new inspiration, he climbed up a hill and began flapping his rather large wings - only to find out that they lifted him off the ground. After further practice, he rose up into the air and began to take flight. Before long, he was met by other eagles who flew off with him to their nesting grounds - finally, the eagle he was created to be.

In a rather simplistic way, this story illustrates a significant truth every Christian must realize - we were created as "eagles", but through the sin of Adam, became "turkeys" - and have lived as turkeys in the barnyard our entire lives.

You see, God created you in His image. He breathed His breath into you and gave you life. You are significant to Him; loved by Him, and created to live daily in His awesome presence for all eternity…but sin altered all that.

The "good news" of the gospel is that Jesus came and died, and rose again so that you and I could once again experience His presence and live like the "eagles" we were created to be. Let's unpack that further…

God's Spirit came to dwell in your spirit, and your spirit came alive.

> *But because of his great love for us, God, who is rich in mercy, made us alive with Christ even when we were dead in transgressions—it is by grace you have been saved. (Ephesians 2:4-5)*

Because of this miraculous gift, we are also told that we have become "a new creation".

> *Therefore, if any man be in Christ, he is a new creature: old things are passed away; behold, all things are become new. (2 Corinthians 5:17)*

You are no longer the person you used to be. You still have your same body, and your same soul - but, spiritually, you are a brand new creation - indwelled by the King of Kings, the Almighty, All-Powerful God, Creator of the universe.

Not only are you a new creation, but (because of Jesus) all of the "natural", "carnal", and "sinful" things you have ever thought, said, or done (and ever will) are completely and forever forgiven by God. If that doesn't make you want to worship Him, nothing will.

> *If we confess our sins, he is faithful and just to forgive us our sins, and to cleanse us from all unrighteousness. (1 John 1:9)*

> *"I, I alone, am the one who wipes out your wrongdoings for My own sake, and I will not remember your sins." (Isaiah 43:25)*

> *"Their sins and lawless acts I will remember no more." (Hebrews 10:17)*

As far as the east is from the west, so far has he removed our transgressions from us. (Psalm 103:12)

Look up these verses also: Ephesians 1:7, Daniel 9:9, Isaiah 1:18, Jeremiah 31:34.

The Bible calls this "justification". You will hear Christians use this term to describe the believer's condition of being completely and totally forgiven of all past, present, and future sins. Because Jesus' blood paid the penalty for our sin, it is "just-if-I'd" never sinned. When God looks upon us, He sees the blood of Jesus and not our sinfulness. That is what the Bible means when it says we are "in Christ."

There is therefore now no condemnation for those who are in Christ Jesus. (Romans 8:1)

Is that not amazing? Is that not wonderful? God not only forgives our sins, but He chooses not to remember them. He does not condemn us for them. Because of Jesus, we will never be accountable for them - ever.

If being forgiven isn't enough, you have been adopted by God and are forever His child and a joint heir with Jesus of His eternal kingdom! This unfathomable truth is very difficult for many Christians to fully comprehend.

Many of us, including myself, grew up with a dysfunctional father. Sadly, many suffered with an angry, addicted, and/or abusive father. A great number of believers find it hard to accept the concept of a deeply loving, nurturing, merciful, forgiving, attentive Father as a result of their difficult past. God goes to great lengths in His love letter to us to let us know how He feels about us:

See what great love the Father has lavished on us, that we should be called children of God! And that is what we are! (1 John 3:1)

Because you are his sons, God sent the Spirit of his Son into our hearts, the Spirit who calls out, "Abba, Father." So you are no longer a slave, but God's child; and since you are his child, God has made you also an heir. (Galatians 4:6-7)

> *The Spirit you received does not make you slaves, so that you live in fear again; rather, the Spirit you received brought about your adoption to sonship. And by him we cry, "Abba, Father." (Romans 8:15)*

> *Yet to all who did receive him, to those who believed in his name, he gave the right to become children of God. (John 1:12)*

> *Consequently, you are no longer foreigners and strangers, but fellow citizens with God's people and also members of his household. (Ephesians 2:19)*

If you believe the Bible, you must then believe that you are now a son or daughter of Almighty God. As such, there is nothing or no one who can take that away from you, and you are assured of an eternity in God's heaven with Him.

> *There is nothing you can do to make God love you any more than He already does, and there is nothing you can do to make Him love you any less.*

That one truth, learned late in my Christian walk, was one of the major "game changers" for me as a believer. My image of a father's love had been predicated on performance. If I did what I was supposed to, if I followed the rules - if, if, if. I never really experienced a father's love that was completely unconditional and without "ifs" or "when's".

When I finally embraced the truth that God's love for me was not predicated on ANYTHING, and that my performance could not alter it, it honestly set me free to live for Him and worship Him as never before. I no longer had to tap dance for approval or act a certain way in order to feel like God loved or accepted me. I AM LOVED! Period!

> *The Lord will take delight in you, and in his love, he will give you new life. He will sing and be joyful over you, (Zephaniah 3:17a)*

What freedom that understanding brought to my soul. I pray God will use it also in your life to allow you to experience the Father's forgiveness, mercy, and love as you were created to experience them.

I STAND AMAZED IN THE PRESENCE

I stand amazed in the presence
Of Jesus the Nazarene,
And wonder how He could love me,
A sinner, condemned, unclean.
Refrain:
O how marvelous! O how wonderful!
And my song shall ever be:
O how marvelous! O how wonderful!
Is my Savior's love for me!
For me it was in the garden
He prayed: Not My will, but Thine.
He had no tears for His own griefs,
But sweat drops of blood for mine.
In pity angels beheld Him,
And came from the world of light
To comfort Him in the sorrows
He bore for my soul that night.
He took my sins and my sorrows,
He made them His very own;
He bore the burden to Calvary,
And suffered and died alone.
When with the ransomed in glory
His face I at last shall see,
'Twill be my joy through the ages
To sing of His love for me.
(Charles H. Gabriel, 1905)

KEY TRUTH =

You are a beloved child of Almighty God, completely forgiven and lavishly loved by Him.

Chapter 5

A NEW RESPONSIBILITY

As wonderful as the reality is that you are a new creation and a forgiven child of your Father God, you must also know that with this new status comes new and great responsibility.

Because you are now a child of the King of Kings, and joint heir with Jesus of all that is His, you are royalty. I know you don't feel like or look like it, but the truth is, you are now a son or daughter of the King of heaven. Wherever you go, you represent the King and His kingdom. At home, at work, at school, on a date, in the marketplace, at the gym, at the golf course, or on the pickleball court - everywhere you go, you represent Him.

Quite honestly, that takes some getting used to. As you take time to read and study your Bible, you will discover a world of wisdom and direction for how believers (His children) should conduct themselves. You will learn that our thoughts matter, our words matter, our actions matter - and even our inaction matters.

> *Therefore, we are ambassadors for Christ, God making his appeal through us. (2 Corinthians 5:20)*

So, it matters how you live, how you act, and how you interact with others. People are watching - lost, unsaved people. We are God's kids, and we have been commissioned by Him to tell others about Him and to live our lives in such a way that they will be drawn to Him.

> *Therefore, go and make disciples of all nations, baptizing them in the name of the Father and of the Son and of the Holy Spirit, and teaching them to obey everything I have commanded you. (Matthew 28:19-20)*

If you let Him, God will use you to bring the good news of Jesus to people who do not know Him. Just like you were, they are " dead in their trespasses and sins" (Ephesians 2:1), walk in darkness, and are blinded to the truth of Jesus.

> *When Jesus spoke again to the people, he said, "I am the light of the world. Whoever follows me will never walk in darkness, but will have the light of life." (John 8:12)*

> *You are the light of the world. A town built on a hill cannot be hidden. Neither do people light a lamp and put it under a bowl. Instead, they put it on its stand, and it gives light to everyone in the house. In the same way, let your light shine before others, that they may see your good deeds and glorify your Father in heaven. (Matthew 5:14-16)*

> *The god of this age has blinded the minds of unbelievers, so that they cannot see the light of the gospel that displays the glory of Christ, who is the image of God. (2 Corinthians 4:4)*

God could speak and everyone on earth would be saved, but He chooses to use us, as His children and ambassadors, to be His instruments to share the good news of Jesus with the world. That is a huge and sacred responsibility.

We bring the light of His kingdom into the darkness around us to every place we go and everyone we meet during the day. We also have the responsibility to share His Good News with family, friends, and even strangers as the Lord leads us.

> *Let your light shine before men in such a way that they may see your good works, and glorify your Father who is in heaven. (Matthew 5:16)*

One of the many reasons we need to read and study the Bible is so we will know what we are to share with others and how to live out our lives in front of them. One of the simplest ways to do that is to share our own story of how we came to believe in Him and how our lives have changed since.

One prayer you can pray daily is to ask God to lead you to people who need to hear the good news and give you the courage to share with them. That is a prayer God loves to answer.

KEY TRUTH =

You are God's ambassador and light in a darkened, sinful world. He will use you to draw others to Him if you follow and obey Him.

Chapter 6

SHEDDING THE OLD CLOTHES

Remember, Lazarus awoke from the dead and walked out of his tomb. He was very much alive but was wrapped in spicy, smelly grave clothes. One of the first things you will notice is that you too, are not totally free of your old, dirty, stinky "grave clothes". You are spiritually alive, but you're still clothed with your old selfish way of living.

In Chapter 3, there was an illustration depicting your spirit, soul, and body. When you asked Jesus into your life to be your Lord and Savior, God's Spirit came to reside in your inner being, your spirit. You will also notice that your soul and body remained the same - unchanged by that same Spirit. Think of that soul and body as your grave clothes. The longer you have "worn" them and lived without God's Spirit in your life, the more tightly those clothes are wound around you.

Over those years, you have lived your life for an audience of one - yourself. You and I, and everyone else born in the world, are born with a "me-centeredness". Life is about me - what I want, what I need. Ask any parent of a young toddler, and they will be quick to tell you that selfishness does not need to be taught.

Because of our innate self-focus, we have most likely stepped on a few toes along our journey, ruffled a few feathers, and done things we regret. Those are called "sins". Sins are the thoughts, words, deeds, and attitudes we exhibit as a result of our self-centeredness and lack of God in our lives.

So now, you must cooperate with the process (and it is a process) of unwrapping the garments of your past life and embracing your new one. Both take time, and both require effort and resolve. At the top of the list of priorities is learning to commune with God through reading and studying your Bible. It is so much more than a book of old stories and helpful rules for living. It is truly the voice of your Father God Himself. It is His Word and His love letter to you.

As it is in life, it takes years for a newborn to grow up. In infancy, newborns aren't capable of eating solid food and need milk to grow. The same is true for all of us who are born again. We are infants in the faith.

> *I had to talk as though you belonged to this world or as though you were infants in Christ. I had to feed you with milk, not with solid food, because you weren't ready for anything stronger. (1 Corinthians 3:1b-2a)*

> *As newborn babies, desire the pure milk of the Word, that by it you may grow in respect to your salvation. (1 Peter 2:2-3)*

What "milk" should you drink as a newborn Christian? Peter answers that question very specifically: "the pure milk of the Word". The most important thing you can do as a new believer is to drink in the Word of God. Newborns don't have a few sips in the morning and then not drink again until the next day. They drain an entire bottle when they wake up and then again several times throughout the day. They need it. They crave it. They are desperate for it. It is life.

Without milk, a young child becomes malnourished, stunted, and even ill. With it, they thrive, put on needed weight, build up their bodies, and grow.

Newborn Christians, like newborn babies, don't need steak. You don't need to immediately try and understand the Book of Revelation or take up the study of Greek. You need the "pure milk of the Word".

The Bible itself says that those who are not believers are not capable of understanding God's Word.

> *But the natural man (unbeliever) can't receive the things of the Spirit of God: for they are foolishness unto him: neither can he know them, because they are spiritually discerned. (1 Corinthians 2:14)*

Since you are no longer a "natural" man or woman (unbeliever), you are now capable of understanding what the Bible is saying. What the Bible is saying is critical for your growth and maturity as a Christian. It is oxygen. Reading it, studying it, and memorizing it are the most important things you can do as a follower of Christ. God's Word is your compass, your light, your wisdom. You cannot hope to know how to mature and how to please Him if you don't read His counsel to you.

> *Man shall not live by bread alone, but by every word that comes from the mouth of God. (Matthew 4:4)*

> *For the Word of God is alive and powerful. (Hebrews 4:12)*

> *God's Word is the truth. Anything contrary to it is a lie. (John 17:17; Proverbs 30:5)*

> *Our faith increases as we hear/read His Word. (Romans 10:17)*

> *His Word illuminates our path, showing us where to go. (Psalm 119:105)*

Hearing God through His Word involves reading the Bible differently than you read a regular book. If you're like me, when I read a book, I read it to get to the end. For some reason, I want to finish the book so I can say, "I read that." Maybe it's a feeling of accomplishing something. - BUT - reading God's book is vastly different. If you consider it His divine wisdom and guidance for you, you have to slow down, and ask God as you read, "Lord, what do You want to speak to me in what I am reading today?

Funny this is, I have been reading it for decades, and even though I have read it through several times - I have never "finished" it.

Pause as you read and think about it, and how it applies to you and your current situation, or need.

For example:

> *Husbands, love your wives, just as Christ loved the church and gave himself up for her. (Ephesians 5:25)*

Instead of reading that as simply a declarative sentence, or even a Godly suggestion, stop and ask the Lord - "Am I loving my wife *'just as'* You loved me? Do I give myself up for her, like You did for me? Lord, help me love her like that, and put her needs above my own today."

See the difference? The Author of this book wants your time to be personal, experiential, and conversational.

That is how God can speak to you through His written Word. Take your time and think about how a verse or passage applies to you, and what God wants to say to you through it.

Much of the Bible is story, and much is also history, but even in the stories and the history, God will speak to you and guide you. There is much current wisdom and direction to be gained through the stories of Moses, David, Jonah, Joseph, Nehemiah, and Peter. What are the life lessons God wants to teach you through theirs? God regularly provides wisdom and even answers to your prayers through His dealings with others in the Bible.

You will find, as you spend more time in God's Word, that your grave clothes are unwinding and falling away. You will find your desire for your old lifestyle and old habits growing distasteful. Something inside you, the Spirit of God, is cleaning up your old way of thinking and acting. You don't have to try and do that yourself (you can't by the way), the Spirit will change your life from the inside out.

So, your very first decision as a new believer is to get your Bible and begin a regular routine of reading it. Most Christians believe the best practice is to set aside time early in your day, before life and busyness steal your time and attention, and spend time with His Word. It is critical that you develop the daily discipline of setting aside a dedicated time to commune with the Father by engaging Him in His Word.

But you're too busy, right? The honest answer is 'yes', we are all too busy. Too busy for the most important things. Somehow, we find time to scroll Facebook and Instagram, or not miss our favorite TV show or Netflix series - but far too many believers use 'too busy' as an excuse to neglect the one thing they need most - time with God.

Resist the temptation to just open to Genesis, Chapter 1, and start reading. Genesis is a fabulous Book to spend time in, and you should do that soon, but in the beginning, many people start with the Gospel of John. This will give you a great overview of Jesus' life, sermons, miracles, and more.

Another great place to begin is with the Epistles, ie, Galatians, Ephesians, Philippians, and Colossians in the New Testament. There is a world of truth and wisdom for everyday living there. God's Word is also our primary offensive weapon to use in spiritual warfare, and you need to know how to wield it effectively. (Ephesians 6)

No matter where you start…START. If you miss a day, don't let that throw you off for a week. If you miss a meal, you will soon find a way to eat. You're going to miss some days, but start back immediately to further establish a lifelong habit.

If your church, or Christian community, has a Bible study (Bible Study Fellowship, Community Bible Study, Better Man, Men's Fraternity, and more) - join up and start studying God's Word with fellow believers. You need community and the shared wisdom of other, more mature followers. Jesus told Lazarus' family and friends to "Take off the grave clothes and let him go." (John 11:44) We need fellow believers to help us unwind from our old lifestyle and give us wisdom from their successes and mistakes. (Chapter 9)

If you've ever tried losing weight, you know it takes discipline; it takes time and effort. If you don't make the effort, you don't reap the rewards, right?

The same is very true when it comes to knowing God's Word.

Remember this: *Whoever sows sparingly will also reap sparingly, and whoever sows bountifully will also reap bountifully. (2 Corinthians 9:6)*

The Bible is like a gold mine. The more you dig, the more you find. God's treasure to us is none other than His own words of wisdom, guidance, and advice. Can you imagine? The God of all creation wrote you a letter, filled with divine wisdom and loving counsel - and you have unfettered access to it anytime you want. Why would you ever neglect such a treasure?

If you ever wonder - "Where do I go from here?", "What do I do next?", "What does God want me to do here?' - here is your answer:

Your word is a lamp for my feet, a light on my path. (Psalm 119:105).

KEY TRUTH =

God's Word is oxygen. It's not an app you call up when you need help. It is life.

Chapter 7

TEACH US TO PRAY

Think of someone from history that you would love to have met and actually spoken with. Who comes to mind (besides Jesus)? I'm thinking Adam, Moses, Peter, Abraham Lincoln, Martin Luther, A.W. Tozer, Billy Graham.

It's great to read that person's biography, or personal memoirs, but what if you could actually have a conversation with them? Would you do all the talking? Would you benefit from hearing what they had to say? Would you not be spellbound?

My first memory of prayer was, "Now I lay me down to sleep. I pray the Lord my soul to keep." That was the memorized, nightly prayer my mother taught my brother and me when we were very young. Even as a teenage believer, my concept of prayer was confined to "asking God for stuff."

Later in my Christian walk, I was told that prayer is NOT a monologue, but a dialogue. God not only wishes to hear what is on my mind and what I need (both of which He already knows), but He wants to speak to me as well. Really? Yes - really!

As a father of three wonderful sons, I relish times with my boys, and having the opportunity to talk with them over lunch, on the golf course, or, frankly, anywhere. Now, as grown men with busy families of their own, those times are rare, which makes them more precious. Can you imagine me having an uninterrupted hour with one of them and having him tell me of the many needs in his life and the myriad issues he is dealing with, and me saying NOTHING? He is desperate for advice and counsel, and I sit silent, aloof, and unresponsive.

If that is my heart as an earthly dad, I can't imagine my heavenly Father desiring any less. Learning to hear the voice of our Father is obviously more complicated than sitting across from Him on the porch, but it is no less attainable. Those believers who enjoy such a relationship have learned how to "hear" God speak to them through His Word, through listening in prayer, and through fellow believers.

But, does God ever actually "speak" to His children? As you set aside time to be alone with God, you will develop the ability to "hear" from God.

In Psalm 46:10, God tells us to "Be still, and know that I am God". In John 10:27, Jesus said, "My sheep hear my voice, and I know them, and they follow me".

God speaks all throughout the Old and the New Testament. You will find examples in the Bible of God speaking loudly and softly, through dreams and visions, through prophets, through His creation, and even through circumstances. The question is - are you listening? He will speak to you through His Word, through prayer, through sermons. audio books and podcasts, and even through Christian friends. One caution, however, is if a friend, pastor, author, etc. suggests what they are saying is "God's word for you" - be sure and compare what they are saying with the Word of God to see if it agrees, and also take it to God in prayer before acting on it.

It is nearly impossible to hear from God amid the noise of our current culture. Most of us spend hours each day on our cell phones and scrolling the internet. If we stop that activity long enough, we turn on the television or play computer games. We work long hours, scurry from carpool pickup to sports practice, to pick up fast food for dinner, only to plop in front of the TV or technology after putting the kids to bed. Is it any wonder we don't seem to hear from the God of the universe in the midst of that prayer can be as short and simple as the "Help me" that Peter shouted as he was sinking in the raging sea as he walked on the water toward Jesus. God hears them all and responds to them all. He will always answer His children's prayers. Sometimes, He says "Yes", sometimes "No", and sometimes "Not now, or Wait". If, however, you really desire to learn to hear His voice, you have to learn to develop the practice of carving out specific, quiet time alone in His presence.

Jesus regularly "went away to a solitary place" to pray. Amid his frenzied schedule, the constant assault by church leaders, and the hundreds that begged Him for healing daily, Jesus needed to hear from His Father to know what He was to do/say next.

> *And in the morning, a great while before day, he rose and went out to a lonely place, and there he prayed. (Mark 1:35)*
>
> *And when it was day, he departed and went into a lonely place. (Luke 4:42)*
>
> *But so much the more the report went abroad concerning him; and great multitudes gathered to hear and to be healed of their infirmities. But he withdrew to the wilderness and prayed. (Luke 5:15-16)*
>
> *Now when Jesus heard this, he withdrew from there in a boat to a lonely place apart. But when the crowds heard it, they followed him on foot from the towns. (Matthew 14:13)*
>
> *And after he had dismissed the crowds, he went up on the mountain by himself to pray. When evening came, he was there alone (Matthew 14:23)*
>
> *In these days he went out to the mountain to pray, and all night he continued in prayer to God. (Luke 6:12)*

Jesus was desperate to hear from His Father. He knew the best place to hear Him was away from the noise and the crowds.

Jesus said to them, *"Truly, truly, I say to you, the Son can do nothing of his own accord, but only what he sees the Father doing; for whatever he does, that the Son does likewise. For the Father loves the Son, and shows him all that he himself is doing; and greater works than these will he show him, that you may marvel. (John 5:19-20)*

If you realize that you too, are desperate to hear from Him regarding where to go, what to do, when to do it, your life, as well as your relationship with Him, will be dramatically different.

Most believers seem to pray only when they are asked or reminded, or if they are in a desperate situation. Obviously, you pray there too, but if you really want to walk with God and experience the life He has called you to, you will work to develop the practice and privilege of prayer throughout the day.

There are volumes written about prayer that you should add to your reading schedule. Much is to be learned from the wisdom of men and women who have walked with God for decades, experienced His presence, and heard His voice along the way. A couple of favorite books that come to mind are: <u>The Practice of the Presence of God</u>, by Brother Lawrence, and <u>Walking with God</u>, by John Eldredge.

As with other skills, your growth in any area of your Christian life is directly proportionate to the amount of time you are willing to commit to acquiring it. You can't expect to grow in your knowledge of God's Word if you don't spend large amounts of time immersed in it. You can't become proficient in prayer or in hearing from God unless and until you are willing to spend quality time alone with Him.

It is the time spent in the Word and in prayer that allows the Spirit of God living in you to begin to spread into your soul and begin to influence your thoughts, your will, and your emotions. Those are the vital areas that control your thinking, your words, your actions, and your interactions with the people around you.

Only then will you begin to see growth and maturity in your Christian walk. You and the people closest to you will also begin to notice changes in your countenance, your language, your decisions, and your lifestyle. What they are witnessing is the falling away of your old grave clothes and the emergence of the new creation that is you.

The choice to do these things - as always - is yours to make.

"God speaks in the silence of the heart. Listening is the beginning of prayer,"
~ Mother Teresa

"Prayer is simply a two-way conversation between you and God,"
~ Billy Graham

"The amount of time we spend with Jesus - meditating on His Word and His majesty, seeking His face - establishes our fruitfulness in the kingdom."
~ Charles Stanley

Prayer is not a monologue, but a dialogue; God's voice is the most essential part. Listening to God's voice is the secret of the assurance that He will listen to mine". ~ Andrew Murray

"Satan's greatest weapon is man's ignorance of God's Word". A.W. Tozer

If you have never prayed or been around believers who pray, you may feel like Jesus' disciples early in their ministry -

He was praying in a certain place, and when he ceased, one of his disciples said to him, "Lord, teach us to pray, as John taught his disciples." (Luke 11:1)

Prayer is a learned habit. Our earliest prayers seem to focus on only asking God for help and/or to meet a need in our lives. While God does want to meet our needs, that immature perspective of prayer is similar to that of a personal genie who is supposed to grant your desires when you ask. It doesn't take long in your study of God and His Word to discover that comparison is far from the truth.

As was said earlier, God hears every one of your prayers and even knows what you are going to ask Him before you ask. Unlike a genie who grants all wishes without reservation, God knows you; He knows your future, and He alone knows what is best for you and for your maturity into the image of Christ. He always answers, but His answer may not always be the answer you are expecting. Sometimes, the answer is "far and above anything you can ask or even think" (see Ephesians 3:20).

Jesus told His disciples to 1) address your prayers to God as your Father, 2) invite His kingdom into your situation (which includes His power, wisdom, direction, love, etc.), 3) ask His forgiveness for any sin present in your life (as you are also forgiving anyone who has sinned against you), and 4) ask for Him to deliver you from temptation and the schemes of the enemy. (Matthew 6)

On the heels of that, He exhorts them to persevere in prayer by "asking, seeking, and knocking" until they get an answer (Luke 11:5-10). God knows the right answer, and He knows the proper timing - so, we are to trust His sovereignty and His great love for us.

Your Father knows you are a babe regarding prayer when you are first born again into His family. He doesn't expect you to be eloquent or formal (Thee and Thou), but simply to speak your mind and speak your heart. He loves to hear your prayers and delights to commune with you. He is never too busy or too distracted with other people and issues to listen intently to what is on your heart.

I have also found great comfort in knowing that both Jesus and the Spirit are praying for me, and I know their prayers are powerful.

> *Is it Christ Jesus, who died, yes, who was raised from the dead, who is at the right hand of God, who indeed intercedes for us? (Romans 8:34)*

> *Consequently, he is able for all time to save those who draw near to God through him, since he always lives to make intercession for them. (Hebrews 7:25)*

> *Now in the same way the Spirit also helps our weakness; for we do not know what to pray for as we should, but the Spirit Himself intercedes for us with groanings too deep for words. (Romans 8:26)*

Prayer is a lifestyle developed by a life of desperation. We are reminded in Scripture that we don't know how to pray as we ought (Romans 8:26), that our hearts are deceitful (Jeremiah 17:9), we easily stray from God's path for us (Isaiah 53:6), that we are lovers of ourselves, proud and ungrateful (2 Timothy 3:2) - just to name a few. We cannot follow Jesus in our own strength.

We are desperate for His help in order to live this new life as a Christ-follower. Thankfully, God already knew that and has a masterful plan for that.

> *For God is working in you, giving you the desire and the power to do what pleases Him. (Philippians 2:13)*

God is going to be working in your heart to create not only the desire to please Him, but He will also provide you the ability to walk in a manner that pleases Him and matures you. If Jesus was desperate to hear from His Father to know how to make the thousands of decisions He needed to make, how much more should we realize that we, too, are desperate to hear from Him as well?

Developing a vibrant, powerful, and meaningful prayer life takes time and practice. It is great to read about prayer and even about the prayers of the disciples and other great men and women of the faith, but you still need to practice praying. Like learning a new language, you need to begin to speak audibly to God, and converse with Him as you walk, drive, cook, play, etc. You need to develop a regular and ongoing conversation with your heavenly Father. Like a soldier on a battlefield with a walkie-talkie that stays open to his commanding officer, our all-wise, all-knowing, all-loving Father keeps His line open to us 24/7.

You will discover there are many types or categories of prayer, including:

- Desperation - when facing an immediate and urgent need (Peter sinking in the sea).

- Intercession - crying out to God for the needs of others

- Confession - humbly asking for forgiveness for sin as the Spirit brings any to mind

- Warfare & Deliverance/Freedom - invoking the full power and authority of the kingdom of heaven, and the name of Jesus, against any scheme of the enemy to "kill, steal, and destroy" areas of your life or the lives of others

- Thanksgiving & Praise - expressing your heartfelt thanks for all God has done, for all He is, and for all He is doing in your life. Singing songs of praise and worship is a wonderful form of prayer to God.

- Supplication & Petition - asking for Godly wisdom, direction, strength, and whatever He deems necessary to navigate life's challenges.

No matter what type of prayer you pray ... pray!

Prayer is also a discipline. Since prayer is our lifeline to God, our enemy is determined to keep us from it. He will work overtime to keep us busy and distracted to convince us that a) we're just too busy to find time to pray, or b) God knows what we need anyway, so there is really no reason to pray. He knows that prayer is power; it is our lifeline to the wisdom and power of God Himself, and that scares Satan to death.

Most of us prickle when we hear the word "discipline", but if you have ever sincerely decided to get into shape, or stay on a budget, or become proficient in a sport or skill of any kind, you know it takes discipline. You also know that, with the appropriate discipline, the results are worth the effort.

Begin to simply talk with God as you would anyone you deeply love and respect. Share your thoughts and ask for His. Remember to take time to listen as well as talk. Get used to praying out loud and everywhere you go. Since God promised to "never leave you", He will always be there, ready, willing, and able to advise, instruct, and lead.

I will put a sample prayer in Appendix A for you as a simple model you can use to begin developing your own conversation with the Father.

Again, the exhortation is this ...PRAY.

Engage with your Father and develop this crucial habit, vital for your spiritual maturity.

KEY TRUTH =

God longs to be involved in every aspect of your life - if you will let Him. Talk with Him. Pray.

Chapter 8

TELL ME ABOUT BAPTISM

You may have already read or heard about believers being baptized. You may have been ceremonially baptized or "dedicated" as an infant or young child. Let's take a minute to explain what baptism is and what it isn't, so you will be better able to move forward with this significant decision.

Why is baptism important anyway? Let's look at what the Bible says:

JESUS' EXAMPLE - *One day, Jesus came from Nazareth in Galilee, and John baptized Him in the Jordan River. As Jesus came up out of the water, He saw the heavens splitting apart and the Holy Spirit descending on Him like a dove. (Mark 1:9-10)*

JESUS' COMMAND - *Therefore, go and make disciples of all nations, baptizing them in the name of the Father, and of the Son, and of the Holy Spirit, and teaching them to obey everything I have commanded you. (Matthew 28:19)*

Jesus, even though he had no sin, set the example for all who were to follow Him by leading the way in submitting to be baptized. Before He ascended into heaven, He commanded His followers to make disciples and baptize them. You will find many other Scriptures relating to baptism, such as Acts 2:38 & 41, Acts 8:12 & 36, Acts 9:18, Acts 16:33, Acts 18:8, & Romans 6:4, to name a few.

So, what is it?

Water baptism is a public declaration of your faith in Jesus Christ and the outward demonstration of the inward transformation that took place when you received Him as your Lord and Savior.

Water baptism is symbolic of Jesus' death, burial, and resurrection. As you are immersed in the water (representing the grave), your old self dies and is buried just as Jesus died and was buried. Then, in the same way Jesus rose to life again, you too rise from the water symbolizing your having new life in Him as a brand new creation. This immersion and rising again is a powerful depiction of your old, sinful life being buried under the atoning blood of Jesus, and you then becoming a new creation, free from the slavery to and penalty of sin. Your old life of darkness and separation from God is discarded and replaced with His light and eternal life in the family and blessing of God.

> *We were therefore buried with him through baptism into death in order that, just as Christ was raised from the dead through the glory of the Father, we too may live a new life. (Romans 6:4)*

> *Therefore, if anyone is in Christ, the new creation has come: The old has gone, the new is here! (2 Corinthians 5:17)*

So, baptism is an act of obedience by a new believer. It is a tangible illustration of Jesus' death, burial, and resurrection, as well as a demonstration to everyone in attendance that you too have spiritually died, been buried with Christ, and raised as a new creation in Christ. It is your first public testimony that serves to announce to the world that you are a new creation - a believer in Jesus Christ.

> *If it's an initiation ritual you're after, you've already been through it by submitting to baptism. Going under the water was a burial of your old life; coming up out of it was a resurrection, God raising you from the dead as he did Christ. When you were stuck in your old, sinful, dead life, you were incapable of responding to God. God brought you alive - right along with Christ! Think of it! All sins forgiven, the slate wiped clean, that old arrest warrant canceled and nailed to Christ's Cross. (Colossians 2:12-14 MSG)*

What baptism is not.

Baptism is not salvation. Baptism doesn't save you, and the lack of baptism doesn't mean you aren't saved. While baptism was commanded by Jesus and an integral part of the conversion of early believers, it was never required as a condition of their salvation.

Baptism is not simply a religious ceremony or a cleansing ritual that needs to be repeated. Many believers have been water baptized (immersed) after discovering they were simply "dedicated" as an infant or sprinkled with water as a child.

I was sprinkled by my Methodist minister as a young teen, even before accepting Jesus as my Savior. Several of my teen friends were doing it, so I didn't want to be left out, and my mother wanted me to. A few years later, as a junior in high school, I accepted Christ as my Lord and committed to follow Him. There was no further discussion of or inclination toward baptism…until.

A few years later, while working as a youth pastor at a small, local church, I felt God leading me to follow Jesus' example of being baptized by being immersed in water, not sprinkled, as a public testimony of my decision to follow Christ.

You may hear the terms "believer's baptism" or "Biblically baptized" used in reference to baptism, so you should be familiar with what those mean. In Jesus' day, when people spoke of baptism, by definition, they assumed someone would be immersed or submerged in water - because….

- The Hebrew word *tevilah* also means to be immersed in water. (John the Baptist was also known as John the Immerser).

- The Greek word in the Bible for baptism is *baptizo*, which literally means to "immerse, to submerge, and to overwhelm".

Jesus is our primary example of being immersed by John, but there are many more examples where the same Greek words are used:

> As soon as Jesus was baptized, <u>he went up out of the water</u>. At that moment, heaven was opened, and he saw the Spirit of God descending like a dove and lighting on him. (Matthew 3:16)

KEY TRUTH =

Biblical baptism is a reminder to you, and a testimony to the watching world, of your new identity in Jesus. It is an act that symbolizes who you are.

Chapter 9

EVERYBODY NEEDS A BODY

Another significant component of maturing in your Christian life is finding your role in the "body of Christ." As a believer in Christ, you are now part of something much bigger than yourself. The Bible calls it "the body of Christ", or His church.

> *Just as a body, though one, has many parts, but all its many parts form one body, so it is with Christ. (1 Corinthians 12:12)*

> *For just as each of us has one body with many members, and these members do not all have the same function, so in Christ we, though many, form one body, and each member belongs to all the others. (Romans 12:4-5)*

As a Christian, you are now automatically a part of a larger body of believers. You may not currently be a member of a local church, or you may have had a bad experience with a church or a church member in your past. Whatever your situation, you are called to become an active, contributing part of a local body of believers. As His child, God has also bestowed on you valuable gifts and talents, and He expects you to use them.

> *Each of you should use whatever gift you have received to serve others, as faithful stewards of God's grace in its various forms. (1 Peter 4:10)*

You may have been given the gift of teaching, or accounting, or administration, or serving, or music, or any number of other things, and God now wants you to use those gifts to glorify Him and to help bless and build His church. Obviously, you can't share those gifts with the church if you aren't a part of one.

Some well-meaning believers I have met in recent years hold the belief that they don't really need the local church. They feel that they are a member of the worldwide church and don't need to meet together with other believers regularly, and especially in a building on Sunday. The Bible seems very clear to me that the opposite is quite true. Each member needs the other, and the church is not going to grow as it should without every believer sharing their gifting with the others.

Yes, God does not need buildings, and yes, *"wherever two or three believers are gathered, He is in their midst" (Matthew 18:20)* - but the Word still says the following:

> *Even so, the body is not made up of one part but of many. Now, if the foot should say, "Because I am not a hand, I do not belong to the body," it would not for that reason stop being part of the body. And if the ear should say, "Because I am not an eye, I do not belong to the body," it would not for that reason stop being part of the body. If the whole body were an eye, where would the sense of hearing be? If the whole body were an ear, where would the sense of smell be? But in fact God has placed the parts in the body, every one of them, just as he wanted them to be. If they were all one part, where would the body be? As it is, there are many parts, but one body.*
>
> *The eye cannot say to the hand, "I don't need you!" And the head cannot say to the feet, "I don't need you!". On the contrary, those parts of the body that seem to be weaker are indispensable, and the parts that we think are less honorable we treat with special honor. And the parts that are unpresentable are treated with special modesty, while our presentable parts need no special treatment. But God has put the body together, giving greater honor to the parts that lacked it, so that there should be no division in the body, but that its parts should have equal concern for each other. If one part suffers, every part suffers with it; if one part is honored, every part rejoices with it. Now you are the body of Christ, and each one of you is a part of it. (1 Corinthians 12:14-27)*

God tells us that we need the fellowship, friendship, encouragement, wisdom, accountability, prayers, and love of our fellow brothers and sisters. Speaking from decades of personal experience, I can assure you this is true. Our closest friends and most loyal prayer warriors have been fellow believers in our church body.

Life is hard - and you are going to need other people in your corner, encouraging you, challenging you, and praying for you.

The encouragement here is for you to seek out and find a Bible-believing, Bible-teaching church to become a member of. And don't be that person who sits in the back row and avoids "getting involved" with this new group of people.

Volunteer to do something. Greet people at the door, help with the parking crew, assist in the coffee shop, join a Bible study, Sunday school class, or small group, just get involved! This is the fastest way to get to know people and assimilate into the church body. The faster you do that, the faster you will feel a part, and understand why the Bible encourages you to do it.

And remember: God expects you to use the gifts and talents He has given you to build up and bless His body, the church, and to glorify Him. If you aren't doing that, you are a) refusing to follow God's design for His church; b) depriving His body of the blessing they will receive from the gifts God has given you, and c) demonstrating to God that you are ungrateful for the gifts/talents He has given you. None of these options is very pleasing to Him.

> "We are created for community,
>
> fashioned for fellowship,
>
> and formed for family,
>
> and none of us can fulfill God's purposes by ourselves."
>
> *Pastor Rick Warren*

KEY TRUTH =

One of the fastest ways to grow in your Christian life is to become a part of a group of like-minded people, zealous to know and walk with God.

Chapter 10

WHAT COULD GO WRONG?

You are a new creation in Christ. Your spirit has come alive; you have been adopted into God's family; you have been given eternal life and a share in Jesus' inheritance; you are royalty and have been given authority; your eyes have been opened to the truth of Scripture; your former "heart of stone" has become a "heart of flesh"; you have the presence, wisdom, and power of God living inside you. What could go wrong?

What most believers realize soon after accepting Christ as their Savior and venturing out into their new lives in Him is that they experience a strange, new struggle. They wrestle with still having or desiring old habits and thought patterns. Their lives don't automatically and magically change into passionate, holy, sinless Christians.

What is happening is that you are experiencing conflict. Your spirit is alive because the Holy Spirit has come to reside there from now on. Your old, dead spirit has been replaced with the "same Spirit that raised Christ from the dead", a powerful, wise, and loving Spirit. The problem is that your old mind (way of thinking), will (self-focus), and emotions (feelings and interactions) were not also resurrected anew. They are still very much alive and are pretty set in their old ways. The older you are when you become a believer, the longer your soul has been in charge of your life and has developed deeper roots into your thinking and behavior.

You will almost immediately sense the conflict raging in your mind. Since our mind controls our actions (our body's responses), we feel conflicted about what we are thinking, or feeling, or how we are reacting to things. Here are some of the conflicts I faced as a new teenage believer:

- All teens want to fit in; they want to be popular, liked, and part of the "in crowd". After accepting Christ, some of my *friends* began to act differently around me, sort of aloof. I didn't get invited to some things and was left out of some things that I would have normally been very much involved in. That sorta hurt my feelings, but I felt like God was pleased that I was changing, and my true friends saw the changes.

- Some of the girls I was attracted to beforehand were now not so attractive. I wasn't sure what to think about that. Oddly, they were just as physically attractive, but something about them had now become unappealing.

- My desire to drink alcohol didn't vanish away, but still hung on - mainly as a part of that whole "fitting in" thing. That led to feeling like a hypocrite for drinking yet trying to live a Christian lifestyle that I presumed didn't include drinking. For the first time in my young life, I felt conviction/guilt for drinking, and for caring more about what my friends thought than what the Lord thought.

There were dozens of other conflicts and battles that seemed to frequent my thoughts. It was like there was a war going on in my soul.

Well, guess what? There was. I just didn't understand it.

> *Peter reminds believers that our sinful desires (passions of our body) wage war against your soul. (1 Peter 2:11)*

> *So I find this law at work: Although I want to do good, evil is right there with me. For in my inner being I delight in God's law; but I see another law at work in me, waging war against the law of my mind and making me a prisoner of the law of sin at work within me. What a wretched man I am! Who will rescue me from this body that is subject to death? Thanks be to God, who delivers me through Jesus Christ our Lord! So then, I myself in my mind am a slave to God's law, but in my sinful nature a slave to the law of sin. (Romans 7:21-25)*

Peter and Paul (and all believers in fact) knew well the battle that goes on between your old self and the new you. Truth is, your old self enjoyed sin and wants to still remind you of its pleasures, while your new nature desires to walk in God's ways and with a desire to please Him. The Spirit in you works daily to lead you closer to God (and His holiness) and away from your former slavery to sin (unholiness).

The good news is, you now have the Spirit in you to lead you and convict you when you begin to go off course. You will experience an inner feeling of "pause", or "not so fast" when presented with options that might compromise your desire to move toward holiness. This conviction is God's way of protecting you and helping you mature as a believer. But, as always, He doesn't force you in one direction or another. He gives you the power of free will. You get to choose which direction to head.

You feel drawn toward (inclined, tempted) going out with the guys for drinks after work, even though you know it may tempt you to join them in a round of drinks (or two). You don't want to be the "party pooper" friend. Your spirit says, "Think about this, is this the best thing for you to do?" and you feel conflicted in the moment. You have to make a choice.

One of my big battles as a married man with a wonderful wife and three young sons was the draw toward (temptation) spending money we didn't have on gifts, trips, etc., for my family. While the intent was noble, we simply didn't have the money, and the main driver in my heart was a desire to "keep up with the Joneses" (whose families were always going on trips and buying new toys). I wanted my family to have those things too. If I were honest with myself, what I really wanted was to feel successful and "as successful" as other friends of mine.

You may already be familiar with this ongoing conflict between living like the old you or choosing to live like the new you. Let me assure you that conflict continues, and the sooner you learn to hear God's voice and follow His leadership, the more mature you will become, and the more joyful your life will be.

And now, we need to unveil the real source behind this battle and introduce you to how best to fight and win these ongoing conflicts.

KEY TRUTH =

Even though you are a new creation with the Spirit of God living in your spirit, your old, sinful way of life still permeates your soul and wants to continue to ruin your life. This conflict is primarily fought on the battlefield of your mind.

Chapter 11

SHOTS FIRED!

What you are about to read is one of the most important truths you must understand. Sadly, it is greatly misunderstood, under-emphasized, and even avoided by many churches and believers. Since I have written an entire book on the subject "Victorious", I will try to cover the highlights for you here. I would encourage you greatly to read and study more about this most important and powerful truth.

> *As a result, the dragon was enraged at the woman and went away to make war on the rest of her children—those who keep the commandments of God and hold fast to the testimony of Jesus. (Revelation 12:17)*

We are at war! As a Christian, you must realize that you are now at war. You did not get a ticket on a cruise ship headed for heaven when you got saved; you enlisted in God's army and were given armor, issued weapons, and commissioned to use them. Here is a small sample of the truths you need to know concerning this:

> *For though we live in the world, we do not wage war as the world does. The weapons we fight with are not the weapons of the world. On the contrary, they have divine power to demolish strongholds. We demolish arguments and every pretension that sets itself up against the knowledge of God, and we take captive every thought to make it obedient to Christ. (2 Corinthians 10:3-5)*

Put on the full armor of God, so that you can take your stand against the devil's schemes. For our struggle is not against flesh and blood, but against the rulers, against the authorities, against the powers of this dark world and against the spiritual forces of evil in the heavenly realms. Therefore, put on the full armor of God, so that when the day of evil comes, you may be able to stand your ground, and after you have done everything, to stand. Stand firm then, with the belt of truth buckled around your waist, with the breastplate of righteousness in place, and with your feet fitted with the readiness that comes from the gospel of peace. In addition to all this, take up the shield of faith, with which you can extinguish all the flaming arrows of the evil one. Take the helmet of salvation and the sword of the Spirit, which is the word of God. (Ephesians 6:11-17)

I have given you authority to trample on snakes and scorpions and to overcome all the power of the enemy; nothing will harm you. However, do not rejoice that the spirits submit to you, but rejoice that your names are written in heaven." (Luke 10:19-20)

It is very obvious in reading the New Testament that we live in a world at war. Because of this, God has provided His children with everything we need to not only fight it but to win. In fact, one of the primary reasons Jesus came to earth was to win the war on our behalf and to disarm our mortal enemy.

The reason the Son of God appeared was to destroy the devil's work. (1 John 3:8b)

And having disarmed the powers and authorities, he made a public spectacle of them, triumphing over them by the cross. (Colossians 2:15)

Jesus' birth, life, death, and resurrection were the death of Satan's rule over the lives of God's people and the beginning of Satan's final judgment and banishment to the pit of hell at "the end of the age".

And the devil, who deceived them, was thrown into the lake of burning sulfur, where the beast and the false prophet had been thrown. They will be tormented day and night forever and ever. (Revelation 20:10)

The diabolical enemy of every believer knows his time is short, and he also knows that he cannot take away our eternal salvation. Therefore, his strategy is to make our lives a living hell, to distract and disrupt our lives, and to destroy everything and everyone we hold dear. That is why the lives of most believers don't look much different from the lives of non-believers.

Christians are not immune to the harassment and torment of anxiety, depression, fear, anger, and even suicide.

> *The thief (Satan) comes only to steal and kill and destroy; I have come that they may have life, and have it to the full. (John 10:10)*

Our enemy works relentlessly, 24/7/365, to rob Christians of their joy, their peace, and their promised abundant life, and you don't have to look very hard to determine that he is doing a good job of it. He works to destroy believers' lives, marriages, children, finances, health, and anything else he can. He can even get a believer so fearful, so hopeless, and so depressed that they will attempt suicide.

Why would a Christian allow this carnage to overtake their life? My answer is - they don't know, or don't truly believe, that they are God's beloved children and have been given divine power, weapons, and authority to overcome every scheme of the enemy in their lives.

Even though most believers have heard bits and pieces about this war or references of an 'enemy' during a sermon or in their reading of the Bible, they have no practical experience dealing with the enemy. The Bible speaks clearly about this struggle by referring to the "hand-to-hand combat" believers engage in regularly in Ephesians 6:12, but most believers are not actively "wrestling" and are getting overwhelmed and defeated by the enemy.

I assure you, if you will take the time to learn about our enemy and his schemes (see 2 Corinthians 2:11), and equip yourself with the truth of the Word regarding our superior position in battle and divine weaponry, you will be able to rise above the battered and bruised Christian life experienced by many, and walk in victory over the enemy.

As always, the decision to "put on the whole armor of God" (Ephesians 6:11) and to use the weapons and authority given to you by Jesus' death and resurrection (2 Corinthians 10:4) is yours to make. This is not a one-time decision, however. You will need to make it every day of your life from here on because the enemy will not stop his pursuit to derail and destroy you (1 Peter 5:8).

He is not to be feared but respected as a powerful foe. He is watching and waiting for any available opportunity to make you stumble and fall. So be alert. Stay on guard, and deal with him at the very first sign of his presence and activity.

> *Above all else, guard your heart, for everything you do flows from it. (Proverbs 4:23)*

> *If I have forgiven anything, I did so for your sakes in the presence of Christ, so that no advantage would be taken of us by Satan, for we are not ignorant of his schemes. (2 Corinthians 2:10-11)*

> *Be careful—watch out for attacks from Satan, your great enemy. He prowls around like a hungry, roaring lion, looking for some victim to tear apart. (1 Peter 5:8)*

> *The weapons we fight with are not the weapons of the world. On the contrary, they have divine power to demolish strongholds. (2 Corinthians 10:4)*

A frequent ploy of the enemy is to whisper words of doubt and shame in your mind whenever you fall short of living like you know you are supposed to. As "the accuser of the brethren," he stands instantly ready to whisper accusations to us whenever we sin in thought, word, or deed. These whispers often include:

"How can you call yourself a Christian and do that?"

"If you were really saved, you would stop doing/saying those things."

"You're not a Christian, you rarely read your Bible and pray."

"You didn't pray the 'correct' prayer of salvation and aren't really saved at all."

There seems to be an endless supply of untruth, deception, and outright lies in His repertoire. Since he can't change the reality of your eternal salvation, he will work diligently to cast doubt on whether or not you're genuinely saved. Once again, if you aren't completely sure, he will take advantage of your doubt.

In case you have ever doubted whether you are truly saved, or if you said the "right" prayer, etc., be assured that God knows your heart. The thief on the cross didn't pray a prayer at all, yet Jesus told him he would be with him (Jesus) in paradise. (You can also use this as a resource to share with anyone you know who may struggle with the assurance of their salvation as well.

It's best to settle the doubt and draw the proverbial "line in the sand" and never have to even give it the time of day ever again.

KEY TRUTH =

You live in a world at war, but Jesus has given us authority over ALL the power of the enemy, in His name. Learn about it, but more importantly, USE IT.

Chapter 12

THE REAL YOU

You are indeed a new creation. You are born again. You are a child of God and a joint heir with Jesus. Your eternity is secure and cannot be taken away. You are filled with the very Spirit of God. But - there is even more you need to know about yourself.

The following truths are critical for every believer to fully grasp in order to appreciate all Jesus did for them on the cross and to overcome every lie, temptation, accusation, and scheme of our enemy.

I Am Accepted

- *I am a child of God (John 1:12)*

- *God knows me personally (John 10:27-30)*

- *I am Jesus' friend (John 15:15)*

- *I have been justified and sanctified in Christ (Romans 5:1)*

- *I am called according to His purpose (Romans 8:28-30)*

- *I have been bought with a price: I belong to God (1 Corinthians 6:20)*

- *I am a saint (Ephesians 1:1)*

- *I have direct access to God through the Holy Spirit (Ephesians 2:18)*

- *I have been redeemed and forgiven of all my sins (Colossians 1:14)*
- *I am complete in Christ (Colossians 2:10)*

I Am Secure in Christ

- *My name is written in heaven (Luke 10:18)*
- *My sins have been completely and permanently forgiven (Romans 4:7-8)*
- *I have peace with God (Romans 5:1-2)*
- *I have been set free from the law of sin (Romans 6:18)*
- *I am forever free from condemnation (Romans 8:1-2)*
- *The Holy Spirit intercedes for me in accordance with God's will. (Romans 8:26-27)*
- *I am assured that all things work together for my good (Romans 8:28)*
- *I cannot be separated from the love of God (Romans 8:35)*
- *God's Spirit lives in me (1 Corinthians 3:16)*
- *I fight with divinely powerful weapons (2 Corinthians 10:4-5)*
- *Christ has set me free from Satan's bondage (Galatians 5:1)*
- *I am seated with Christ in heavenly places, far above Satan's dominion (Ephesians 2:1-10)*
- *I am confident that God will perfect the good work He has begun in me (Philippians 1:6)*
- *I can do all things through Christ who strengthens me (Philippians 4:13)*
- *I have not been given a spirit of fear, but of power, love, and a sound mind (2 Timothy 1:7)*
- *I can always come before Him to find grace and mercy in time of need (Hebrews 4:16)*
- *Greater is He Who is in me that he that is in the world (1 John 4:4)*

- *If I resist the devil, he will flee from me (James 4:7)*

What I have discovered in my many years as a believer, teacher, speaker, and elder in the church is that most believers don't fully comprehend WHO they are. The problem with that if you don't know WHO you are, you will be more easily deceived by Satan's accusations and lies.

When Jesus was tempted by Satan in the wilderness, the first approach used by Satan was to challenge Jesus' identity.

Then Jesus was led up by the Spirit into the wilderness to be tempted by the devil. And he fasted forty days and forty nights, and afterward, he was hungry. And the tempter came and said to him, "If you are the Son of God, command these stones to become loaves of bread." (Matthew 4:1-3)

"*IF you are the Son of God*"…Satan was attempting to challenge Jesus' true identity. As the "accuser of the brethren" (us), he continues to use the same tactic to keep us from realizing who we really are as God's children, so we won't be able to keep him from his primary mission to "*kill, steal and destroy*" us. (John 10:10)

If, however, believers knew who they really are, that Satan has been defeated, disarmed, and has no power over them, they would begin to enjoy the "abundant life" promised by Jesus in Matthew 16:18 - *upon this rock I will build My church; and the gates of Hell will not stand against it.*

You are royalty.

You have divine authority as a child of Almighty God when dealing with spiritual forces.

You fight spiritual battles with "divinely powerful weapons, and you fight "from" victory, not "for" victory.

You have the "sword of the Spirit", the living, powerful Word of God, to wield as a divinely powerful sword against the lies of the enemy… but you have to know it to use it effectively.

You have the right and authority to invoke the name above all names when dealing with "principalities, powers, and spiritual forces of darkness." That name is JESUS. See how often the disciples invoked the name of Jesus in the Book of Acts,

KEY TRUTH =

You are much more than "just" a Christian. You are a child of the King of Kings, with His authority to defeat all of Satan's schemes. Learn to walk like who you are.

Chapter 13

TIME TO CHANGE CLOTHES

As the grave clothes of your old life continue to fall away, the Bible exhorts you to take off (put off) other things from your old way of life…

> *<u>Put off</u> your old self, which is being corrupted by its deceitful desires; to be made new in the attitude of your minds; and to put on the new self, created to be like God in true righteousness and holiness. (Ephesians 4:22-24)*
>
> *<u>Cast off</u> the works of darkness (Romans 13:12a)*
>
> *Therefore, since we are surrounded by so great a cloud of witnesses, let us also <u>lay aside</u> every weight, and sin which clings so closely, and let us run with perseverance the race that is set before us. (Hebrews 12:1)*

It is our responsibility to "put off/take off" all the remnants of our old life that are in our power. We can't just take off our old self like an old shirt, cast it aside, and never see it again. Many of the habits and hangups from our past want to linger, and if we're honest, we often feel comfortable hanging on to many of them, like that soft old pair of jeans or the tattered sweatshirt we can't seem to throw out.

Frequently, when a Christian finds they are continually plagued by evil forces or by sinful habits they seem to not be able to overcome, the reason lies in their not putting off one or more old habits or sins they are hanging on to, ie: the afternoon cocktail to help you "unwind", the vulgar television series that you justify watching because you like the characters or the storyline, or the gawking at scantily-clad women online because you think "you deserve it", or that "it doesn't hurt anyone". The list is endless.

Many believers, and their children, are tormented by nightmares and irrational fear until they decide to rid their homes of evil television shows, movies, and video games.

As exterminators will tell you, the best way to rid your home of rats is to get rid of their food. If they have no food to indulge in, they will get frustrated and move on to someone else's home. If Christians want to rid their lives (and those of their kids) of the presence of ongoing evil, they need to ask God to reveal to them any "food" that may be keeping them around. If any of the following are food for the temptations, fears, anxieties, etc., that take you and your family to continue to fall victim to, get rid of them:

- Alcohol, drugs, tobacco products, etc.
- Sexually explicit TV, movies, games or internet, books, music
- Sexually inappropriate or provocative TV, movies, games, internet, books, games, music
- Horror, evil, Satanic, demonic, occult TV, movies, games, internet, books, games, music
- Vulgar, anti-Christian, TV, movies, games, internet, books, games, music

God may reveal others to you if you take the initiative to ask Him and take the time to listen. Once He reveals something to you, it is your responsibility to "put off" those things. Many believers have seen immediate and profound freedom when they clean out the food that gives the "rats" permission to remain in their lives.

One of the most prevalent and destructive "foods" that Christians allow that keeps them in bondage for years is unforgiveness. One of the most powerful things you can do as a believer at any age and stage of maturity is to ask God to help you identify every person from your past (and your present) who has said or done anything that offended or hurt you. That could potentially be a long list, but take the time to make it.

The people on that list hold great influence and power over your life, whether you know it or not. Their demeaning and hurtful words or actions created deep bruises in your soul that you carry with you today. With God's leading and His help, you can let go of the natural inclination for revenge or payback and, as an act of your will, and not your emotions, forgive them.

Only God is capable of giving you the grace and mercy to finally "put off" any unforgiveness that remains in your heart. By obeying God in this, you begin to not only "put off" your old self but to begin to "put on" your new self. In case you have that "I don't really want to" attitude about forgiveness. It is a command from the Lord, so you'd better think again.

It doesn't matter how you feel, or whether you think the offending person(s) deserve it - it is an act of your will to let it go and give it to Him.

- *For if you forgive men their trespasses, your heavenly Father also will forgive you; (Matthew 6:14)*

- *And whenever you stand praying, forgive, if you have anything against anyone; so that your Father also who is in heaven may forgive you your trespasses." (Mark 11:25)*

- *be kind to one another, tenderhearted, forgiving one another, as God in Christ forgave you. (Ephesians 4:32)*

Offering someone forgiveness is one major step you can take toward maturity. Forgiveness is a practice that you will need to follow from now on in your Christian walk. People will disappoint you, let you down, hurt your feelings, etc., and you will have to decide whether you are going to harbor those hurts or obey God and let them go. Let God deal with those people as He sees fit. He's much better at it anyway!

Other parts of your new spiritual "wardrobe" to put on include:

> <u>Put on</u> *the full armor of God, so that you can stand against the devil's schemes (Ephesians 6:11)*

Do not lie to each other, since you have <u>taken off</u> your old self with its practices and have <u>put on</u> the new self (Colossians 3:9-10)

Therefore, as God's chosen people, holy and dearly loved, <u>clothe yourselves</u> with compassion, kindness, humility, gentleness, and patience. (Colossians 3:12)

"And above all these <u>put on</u> love, which binds everything together in perfect harmony" (Colossians 3:14)

This practice of taking off and putting on is also an ongoing pursuit. About the time you think you have made great strides in one area, God reveals a different area that needs work. This process is what is called "sanctification", which is the progressive work of the Holy Spirit to make a believer more like Jesus.

Other definitions say it this way:
    The process of being set apart for God's use, or made holy.
    The outworking of the Holy Spirit in a person's life.
    The process of being freed from sin and conformed to the likeness of
    Christ.

Basically, sanctification is the ongoing process of cooperating with the Holy Spirit's working in us in taking off the grave clothes of our old life of sin and putting on the character of our Lord Jesus.

As always, the Spirit does not do this work without our consent and cooperation. As you submit to His leadership, you will find He is changing you from the inside out, and that is a change you will welcome greatly.

- *Do not be conformed to this world, but be transformed by the renewal of your mind, that you may prove what is the will of God, what is good and acceptable and perfect. (Romans 12:2)*

The new birth is not simply the start of a new life,
but the end of the old. God does not patch up the old man;
He makes a new man.
~ A.W. Tozer

Our old history ends at the cross;
our new history begins with the resurrection.
~ Watchman Nee

Let us not then cling to the old garments,
nor seek to put patches on them,
but let us cast them off entirely,
and put on the new robe which Christ has given us.
~ John Chrysostom (4th century)

KEY TRUTH =

By spending time in God's Word, you will discover what needs to be "put off" and what needs to be "put on" to allow the Spirit the opportunity to "sanctify" you from the inside out and become transformed - more like Jesus.

Chapter 14

LET YOUR LIGHT SHINE

To recap…before you accepted Jesus as your Savior, you were lost, without hope, separated from God, spiritually dead in your trespasses and sins, a citizen of the kingdom of darkness.

Spiritually speaking, your spirit was dead, and you walked in darkness, not knowing you were under the power and domain of the ruler of that dark kingdom - Satan. You, me, and everyone born after Adam's sin are born this way. In that darkness, you cannot see where you're going and have no idea how to get out of it, nor do you care to.

But God, out of His great love for you, pursued you, called you in that darkness, and you heard His voice and responded. You became alive spiritually for the very first time and, like Lazarus, walked out into the light. Unlike Lazarus' physical tomb, you walked out of a spiritual tomb and into His "marvelous light".

There is one other gift that you received in that eternity-changing process because the One Who took up residence in your spirit is none other than God Himself - you were filled with His light, literally. Spiritual beings, both good and evil, can now see the light emanating from you. Angels know who you are, and demons know who you are - because your light shines brightly in the deep darkness of this world we live in. Here is a little of what God says about that:

> *But you are a chosen people, a royal priesthood, a holy nation, God's special possession, that you may declare the praises of him **who called you out of darkness into his wonderful light.** (1 Peter 2:9)*

*When Jesus spoke again to the people, he said, "I am the light of the world. Whoever follows me will never walk in darkness, but will **have the light of life**." (John 8:12)*

*For at one time you were darkness, but now **you are light in the Lord**. **Walk as children of light.** (Ephesians 5:8)*

*"**You are the light of the world**. A city set on a hill cannot be hidden. Nor do people light a lamp and put it under a basket, but on a stand, and it gives light to all in the house. In the same way, **let your light shine before others**, so that they may see your good works and give glory to your Father who is in heaven. (Matthew 5:14-16)*

*The **light of the righteous** shines brightly. (Proverbs 13:9)*

*In him was life, and the life was **the light of men**. (John 1:4)*

Think about this - "YOU are light". In the spiritual, unseen world, you are light, a bright light shining in the pitch darkness around you. Wherever you go, you bring light. Have you ever been in a pitch-dark environment, like the woods at night, or a cave, or anywhere where you literally can't see your hand in front of your face?

What happens when someone lights a match or turns on a flashlight in a dark room? All the darkness vanishes in a flash. Can you imagine what happens in the presence of God's light?

Natural darkness flees in the presence of light. Spiritual darkness flees in the presence of spiritual light as well.

*The light shines in the darkness, and the **darkness has not overcome it.** (John 1:5)*

What are we supposed to "do" with this divine light?

That you may be blameless and innocent, children of God without blemish

> *in the midst of a crooked and twisted generation, among whom **you shine as lights in the world.** (Philippians 2:15)*

> ***To open their eyes**, so that they may turn from darkness to light and from the power of Satan to God, that they may receive forgiveness of sins and a place among those who are sanctified by faith in me.' (it was Paul's mission to shine the light of Christ into the darkness (lostness) of the Gentile nation - and it is ours as well). (Acts 26:18)*

God calls each of us to take the light inside us into the "crooked and twisted generation" among whom we live, with the mission to "open their eyes so that they may turn from darkness to light". That is a significant and sober responsibility.

We carry God's light into our world not only to dispel the darkness set against us personally, but more importantly, to bring light into the heavy, tormenting darkness haunting the lives of family, friends, colleagues, and even strangers who the Lord brings into our lives.

> *For at one time you were darkness, but now **you are light in the Lord. Walk as children of light.** (Ephesians 5:8)*

Wherever you are, wherever you go, you carry the light of God. You are royalty, a child of the King of Kings, filled with His Spirit. You are NOT a "poor sinner, saved by grace". That describes the OLD you. You are now a SAINT, a righteous child of God, who occasionally sins. You carry the weight of responsibility to represent Him well to the world around you.

> *For we are God's handiwork, created in Christ Jesus to do good works, which God prepared in advance for us to do. (Ephesians 2:10)*

> *In the same way, let your light shine before others, that they may see your good deeds and glorify your Father in heaven. (Matthew 5:16)*

> *For I was hungry and you gave me something to eat, I was thirsty and you gave me something to drink, I was a stranger and you invited me in, I needed clothes and you clothed me, I was sick and you looked after me, I was*

in prison and you came to visit me.' "Then the righteous will answer him, 'Lord, when did we see you hungry and feed you, or thirsty and give you something to drink? When did we see you a stranger and invite you in, or needing clothes and clothe you? When did we see you sick or in prison and go to visit you?' "The King will reply, 'Truly I tell you, whatever you did for one of the least of these brothers and sisters of mine, you did for me.' (Matthew 25:35-40)

The Bible tells us that we will not be judged for our sins. Jesus paid the penalty for all of our past, present, and future sins on the cross and covered them with his blood. When God looks at us, He sees the righteousness of His Son. Nothing we ever do will change that.

But Scripture teaches that God will judge believers' works after we die. The believer's judgment, called the Judgment Seat of Christ in 2 Corinthians, is a judgment for the purpose of assigning eternal rewards based on our service to Christ. Paul wrote detailed descriptions of the Judgment Seat moment in three different passages:

Therefore, we also have as our ambition, whether at home or absent, to be pleasing to Him. For we must all appear before the judgment seat of Christ, so that each one may be recompensed for his deeds in the body, according to what he has done, whether good or bad. (2 Corinthians 5:9-10)

But you, why do you judge your brother? Or you again, why do you regard your brother with contempt? For we will all stand before the judgment seat of God. For it is written, "As I live, says the Lord, every knee shall bow to Me, and every tongue shall give praise to God." So then each one of us will give an account of himself to God. (Romans 14:10-12)

According to the grace of God which was given to me, like a wise master builder, I laid a foundation, and another is building on it. But each man must be careful how he builds on it. For no man can lay a foundation other than the one which is laid, which is Jesus Christ. Now if any man builds on the foundation with gold, silver, precious stones, wood, hay, straw, each man's work will become evident; for the day will show it because it is to be revealed with fire, and the fire itself will test the quality of each man's work. If any man's work which he has built on it remains, he will receive a reward. If any man's work is burned up, he will suffer loss; but he himself will be saved, yet so as through fire. (1 Corinthians 3:10-15)

• Other Scriptures include: 1 Samuel 26:23, Matthew 6:19-21, 1 Timothy 6:18-19, Colossians 3:23-24, Ephesians 6:7-8, Matthew 5:11-12, Matthew 6:1-4, Matthew 10:42, Luke 6:35

Letting the light of God shine through us in this dark world is best demonstrated by living our daily lives with a view towards eternity, and towards influencing as many people as we can to join us there. Every good deed, encouraging word, unselfish act, etc., makes a difference - to God and to the recipient. Jesus said, he came "not to be served but to serve" (Matthew 20:28) and "the greatest among you will be your servant" (Matthew 23:11).

As His ambassadors, our lives should reflect his loving, servant attitude and bring his light into every situation we encounter.

KEY TRUTH =

His Spirit brought with Him the very light of God, and you have an ongoing responsibility to take His light into the lost and darkened world around you with the hope to "open their eyes so that they may turn from darkness to light".

Chapter 15

NOW WHAT?

As the old riddle goes, How do you eat an elephant? Answer: One bite at a time.

You are a new believer, filled with the presence and power of Almighty God. You are a new "babe in Christ" and in need of spiritual milk to grow as you should. It is easy to get lost in the many facets involved in understanding and interpreting the language, the definitions, and the whole culture around the church and Christendom.

We have briefly covered quite a bit of that information, and I pray it has made sense to you. My advice would be to begin taking those "bites" beginning immediately in this order:

1. Read and study the Bible. Ask a mature believer you know where they would recommend you begin. Many new believers start with the Gospel of John in order to get an overview of Jesus' life and ministry. The epistles (Galatians, Ephesians, Philippians, and Colossians) are filled with practical wisdom and direction concerning how to live out your faith. Reading a Proverb a day (there are 31) is a great addition to other studies, as each Proverb is full of God's wisdom for living. The bottom line is - START….and Don't Quit.

2. Begin to pray not only every morning but all throughout the day. God's Spirit is always with you (because He is IN you) and desires to be involved in every aspect (big or small) of your life. If you are new to praying, I encourage you to read Matthew 6:9-13, and also check out the "crafted" prayer in **Appendix**

A as a guide to get you started in your pursuit of developing a sincere and authoritative prayer life. Remember - there are prayers of "petition" (seeking God for needs in your own life), prayers of intercession (praying for the needs of others), and prayers of "warfare" (dealing with confronting and overcoming the assaults of the enemy). Each requires a different approach, which you will learn as you mature in your faith.

3. Find a Bible-believing, Bible-teaching, growing church and become an active, contributing member. You need them, and they need you. No "wallflower" approach - stay off the back row and decide to engage early and often.

4. The years ahead of you, the "race set before you," are not a sprint, but an ultramarathon. You will need help to make it and finish well. Find a mature believer who is willing to meet with you regularly to offer his/her years of wisdom and counsel in order to accelerate your growth in Christ. This is another area where being shy is not a great approach. Observe the older men/women around you who have been committed Christians for years and whose lives you admire. Many are more than willing and eager to mentor/disciple someone new in their faith, but find it awkward to approach them as well. Just ask. See what God will do.

5. Read. Carve out time and energy away from social media and TV to read powerful books on living the Christian life. If you're not a reader, see if you can find those books on Audible or other audio resources. Why is this so important?

Set your minds on things above, not on earthly things. (Colossians 3:2)

Those who live according to the flesh have their minds set on what the flesh desires; but those who live in accordance with the Spirit have their minds set on what the Spirit desires. The mind governed by the flesh is death, but the mind governed by the Spirit is life and peace. (Romans 8:5-6)

Do not conform to the pattern of this world, but be transformed by the renewing of your mind. Then you will be able to test and approve what God's will is—his good, pleasing and perfect will. (Romans 12:2)

Your mind is the most important organ in your body. It is also the most important "organ" in your spiritual body. The wisest king ever to rule the Jewish nation, Solomon, said of our mind - "Above ALL things, - guard your heart/mind" (Proverbs 4:3), because "everything you do flows from it".

Start there. Fill your mind with God's Word. It is the foundation from which your entire life will be built. Walk with God moment by moment and enjoy your new life. As Jesus told His disciples in Matthew 4:19: *Follow me, and I will make you.* If you follow Jesus closely, He will be responsible for "making you" into the man or woman He has called you to be.

The Apostle Paul encouraged us to - "run with endurance the race set before us, fixing our eyes on Jesus, the author and perfecter of our faith" (Hebrews 12:1-2). My friend, Robbie Linn, is famous for his quote, "The hardest thing about being a Christ follower is following Christ". Simple, but true. Following takes an ongoing, deliberate effort on our part. We must stay close and make the daily decision to follow wherever He leads us - the rest is up to Him. Your NEXT STEPS begin NOW!

KEY TRUTH =

Your walk as a Christian is a journey. Maturity takes time, but it also takes action. Following Jesus requires that you keep your eyes on Him and take steps each day to go where He is leading.

APPENDIX A

As you read the Psalms, you discover King David prayed honestly and openly to God. At times angry with God, confused by God - but in many more moments, deeply in awe and reverence before Him. He dialogued with God in prayer and had no problem expressing his honest, raw feelings. God knew his heart and his needs before he even prayed, so his forthrightness didn't bother the Father at all.

You see, your heavenly Father is not a "far-off, disinterested, too busy" God, or an angry "Wizard of Oz" God. Instead, He is the most loving, patient, engaging Father you could ever hope for. The Bible even tells us that, as His adopted children, we even have the right to call him "Abba" or "Daddy" (see Romans 8:15, Galatians 4:6).

Your Father knows your heart and your needs. He loves you like no one you have ever known and longs to commune with you every day. Open your heart and talk with Him. It may take time and much practice to open up this way, but it will come if you work at it.

I promised to include a sample prayer that might help provide some simple 'language' as you develop your own open, honest conversation style of dialoguing with God.

Heavenly Father, thank You for loving me and pursuing me. Thank You for including me in Christ, forgiving me all my past sin, and making me complete in Him.

Lord Jesus, I honor you as my Lord, and I surrender every aspect and dimension of my life to You. Thank You for suffering a gruesome death so my sins would be covered by Your blood and forever forgiven.

Holy Spirit, thank You that You reside in me. You have clothed me with power from on high, sealed me in Christ, and become my counselor, comforter, strength, and guide. Fill me afresh today, and help me walk in step with You in all things.

Thank You Father, for meeting all of my needs through Your riches in Christ. I lay all my needs, my fears, my anxiety, and my future at Your feet, knowing You will do "exceedingly, abundantly above all I can ask or think". Help me to rest in You and trust You to lead me in the way I should go. I want Your will for my life, and ask that You help me grow closer to You, to hear Your voice, and follow wherever You lead.

Thank You for Your presence in me and with me today. In the mighty name and authority of Jesus, I pray.

Amen.

SOME FINAL THOUGHTS

The older you are, the more you will come to agree with this statement: ***Life is Hard***.

That was true before you became a believer, and it is even more true now. Not only do you have the typical struggles of life, but now you have a cunning, diabolical, and powerful enemy to deal with in the middle of them.

Family is hard. School is hard. Work is hard. Handling money, bills, and savings is hard. Friendships are hard. Marriage is hard. Kids are hard. Teenage kids are hard. Grown kids and in-laws are hard. Health is hard. Getting old is hard. Death is hard.

As a born-again Christian, you will find that all of these life stages are still hard, sometimes extremely hard. That is why your faith in God, your daily walk with Christ, and your intimate fellowship with devoted Christian friends are so vital. Without them, you are left to find direction, wisdom, answers, support, and comfort on your own.

Becoming a Christian doesn't make "hard" go away. It doesn't automatically make these hard things less hard, but you will find that in Christ, you can actually find the direction, wisdom, answers, support, and comfort you need to navigate them.

I pray this book will serve to jump-start your journey of faith. The decisions you make from here will determine if you grow and mature into a fruitful and fulfilled child of God, or struggle as a part-time follower who feels disconnected from God and unfulfilled in life.

The fellowship of the Father's presence, the wisdom of His Word, along with the deep friendship of fellow believers, will prove to be your anchor, your compass, and your joy in the years ahead.

Run to Him - Listen to Him - Do what He says - and you will finish well.

Other Books by Rob Thorpe

VICTORIOUS
Winning the Spiritual Battles in Your Life

Hand Me Downs
What to do About Generational Iniquity

All In
A Marriage Worth Dying For

CHOICES
10 Decisions That Will Change Your Marriage Forever

"husband" - A User's Guide

www.ingramcontent.com/pod-product-compliance
Lightning Source LLC
Chambersburg PA
CBHW081642040426
42449CB00015B/3427